Ores

by Grace Hansen

abdopublishing.com

Published by Abdo Kids, a division of ABDO, PO Box 398166, Minneapolis, Minnesota 55439.

Copyright © 2016 by Abdo Consulting Group, Inc. International copyrights reserved in all countries.
No part of this book may be reproduced in any form without written permission from the publisher.

Printed in the United States of America, North Mankato, Minnesota.

052015

092015

THIS BOOK CONTAINS
RECYCLED MATERIALS

Photo Credits: iStock, Shutterstock

Production Contributors: Teddy Borth, Jennie Forsberg, Grace Hansen

Design Contributors: Laura Rask, Dorothy Toth

Library of Congress Control Number: 2014958427

Cataloging-in-Publication Data

Hansen, Grace.

 Ores / Grace Hansen.

   p. cm. -- (Geology rocks!)

ISBN 978-1-62970-908-6

Includes index.

1. Ores--Juvenile literature. 2. Mineralogy --Juvenile literature.   I. Title.

553--dc23

                    2014958427

Table of Contents

What Are Ores?

Ores are naturally occurring rocks. These rocks have metal inside them.

4

gold

5

Ore Formation

Ores form from **minerals**. Some minerals form in cooling **magma**. Magma is under the ground.

Magma hardens as it cools.

It sometimes cools slowly.

This forms bigger minerals.

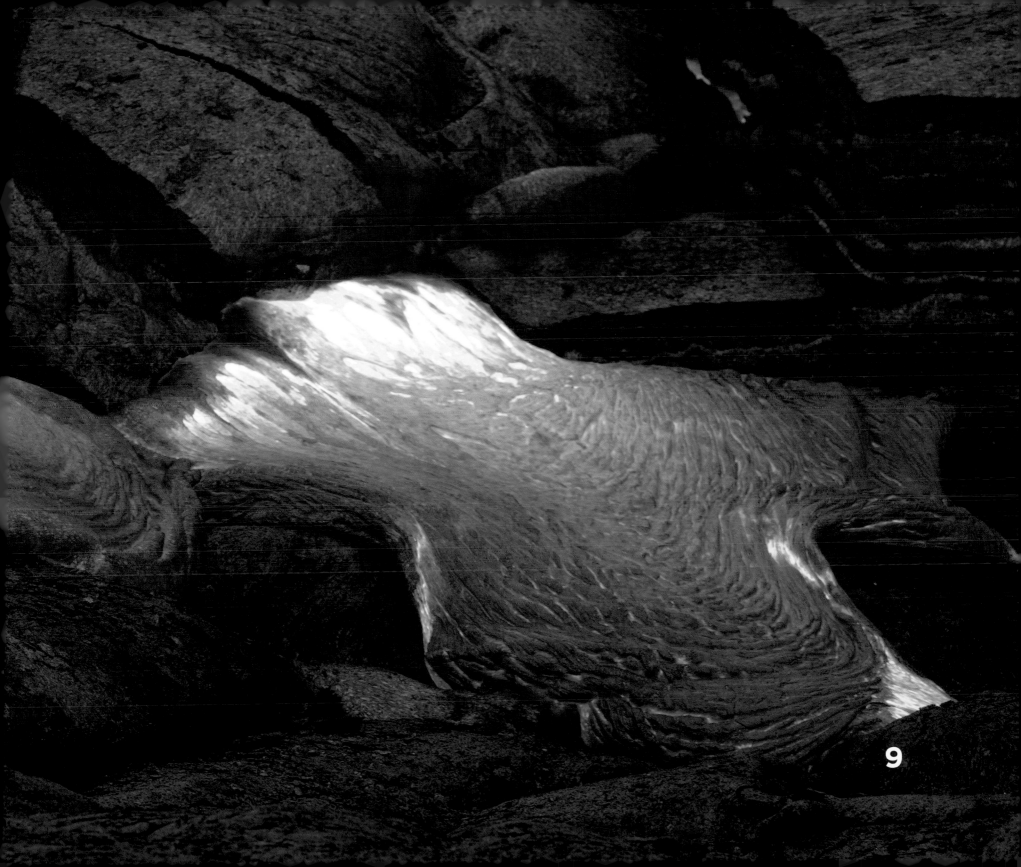

9

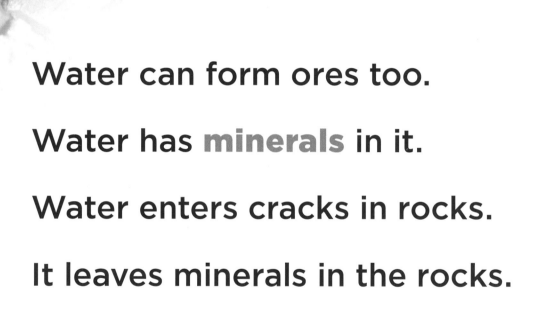

Water can form ores too.

Water has **minerals** in it.

Water enters cracks in rocks.

It leaves minerals in the rocks.

Water also breaks down rock. It moves the pieces somewhere else. These are called placer deposits.

Using Ores

We **mine** ores. We use ores

for the metal inside them.

14

We use metals every day.
Aluminum comes from
ore. It is light. We use
it to make airplanes.

Iron comes from ore. It is strong. We use it to make steel. Steel is used to make buildings.

19

Copper comes from ore.

Copper is a good **conductor**.

We use it in electrical wire.

21

Ore Types

bauxite

copper

hematite

cassiterite

galena

pyrrhotite

cinnabar

gold

rutile

Glossary

conductor – an object that allows electricity or heat to move through it.

magma – melted rock beneath or within Earth's surface. Igneous rock is formed from it. Magma becomes lava once it reaches Earth's surface.

mine – dig in earth for minerals.

mineral – a substance, such as salt, that is naturally formed under the ground. It makes up rocks and other parts of nature.

Index

abdokids.com

Use this code to log on to abdokids.com and access crafts, games, videos, and more!

Abdo Kids Code:
GOK9086